i'd like
to hear
a flower
g r o w.

and other poems by
Phyllis Halloran

Designed and illustrated by: Carol Reynolds

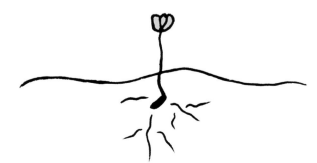

For: My Mother
        Bill
          Beth

Special Thanks to:

Ina

Joanna

Annie

6

O
g r

i'd like to hear a flower g r O W.

I'd like to hear a flower grow,
Or listen to a flake of snow

Taste the scent of morning glories
Sip the fear from spooky stories

See the sound that music makes
Watch the noise of screeching brakes

Smell a rainbow in the sky
Sniff a daydream passing by

Touch imaginary fences.
Good grief! I think I've lost my senses!

wait 'til you hear what i saw

I was fall'n down laugh'n
When I saw a giraffe'n
The middle of the road wearing mittens.

Then a hippo hopped by
In a polka-dot tie
And a polar bear juggl'n some kittens.

A mouse in a hat
Stopped by for a chat
With an ostrich in ballet slippers.

But the silliest thing
I saw by far
Was a seal flipp'n flap jacks with its flippers!

watching squirrels

I am really exhausted
From watching all those squirrels
Run up and down the oak trees
With their tails done up in curls.

Daddy says winter's coming
And squirrels have a lot to do.
They need to gather acorns
For making acorn stew,

And little acorn pizzas,
And acorn pudding cream pies,
Fresh frozen acorn sundaes,
Acorn burgers, acorn fries,

Acorn noodles for their soup,
And sweet acorn muffins, too.
I'd sure get sick of acorns
If I were a squirrel! Wouldn't you?

little black squirrel

There's a little black squirrel
That runs around my yard
Chasing all the other squirrels
And working very hard.

I think in little squirrel talk
He tells them what to do.
Like, "Build a nest! Go gather food!
Move right along, now. Shoo!"

Some of the squirrels stop to play
But never for very long,
Because busy little black squirrel
Gets them moving right along.

He's always very serious,
Though I don't think he gets cross.
He's like a lot of people.
He just wants to be the boss!

it's not fair

I always get the smallest
When there's cake or cookies or pie.

Sometimes I get forgotten
When people are saying good-bye.

All my clothes are hand-me-downs
And they hardly ever fit.

By the time I get out to the car
There's never a place to sit.

I still can't reach the table
So they put me on a cushion.

I'm the one who always gets blamed
Whenever there's any pushin'.

Nobody ever asks me
What I think or if I care.

Being the smallest kid in the family
Is no fun and IT'S NOT FAIR!!

endless

Nobody wants to play with me!
I'ts hard to believe but true.
I'm feeling bad. I'm feeling sad.
What am I going to do?

I sure would like to play baseball,
But I can't do that alone.
Even my dog has deserted me,
So forget about "fetch the bone."

My brother's fixing his junky bike.
My sister's blabbing with her friends.
I just know that this is going to be
A day that never ends.

over and over

The best thing about climbing up a hill

And rolling to the bottom is

when
You get
yourself up,
brush yourself off
And then do it all over again!

worried

Something strange is happening to me.
Nothing about me seems to agree.
My ears are too big. My nose is too long.
My left and right foot don't get along.

My clothes don't fit me suddenly.
Peculiar thoughts are inside of me.
From forehead to chin I'm covered with zits.
This condition I'm in is really the pits!

My parents whisper and stare, you see.
I think they know something's wrong with me.
There they go again. Sh! Listen! Oh, gee!
I knew it! I'm a goner! I've got PUBERTY!?!

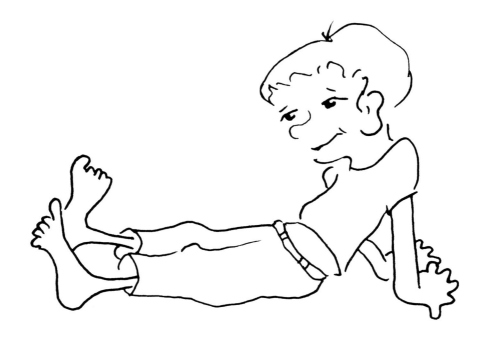

the bee

A bee was perched upon my nose.
I flicked it off onto a rose.
It danced upon the rose's head,
Then flew to a nearby flower bed.

All morning long the bee did prance.
From flower to flower it did its dance.
And just before it flew away
I think the bee was trying to say,

"The dance I do is just for you,
So you can have flowers all year through."
Now every time I see a bee
I know it's dancing just for me.

I am not frightened by the buzz
At all anymore and that's because
Bees are busy dancing, you see,
And hardly have time for stinging me!

easy sharing

The best thing about
The stars we see
Is while they are yours
They belong to me.

The sun and the moon
In the sky of blue
Shine brightly for me
While they shine for you.

The rain that falls,
The grass that grows
The dew that sparkles
The wind that blows

The dark nights that turn
Into days so fair
Are the easiest things
We have to share.

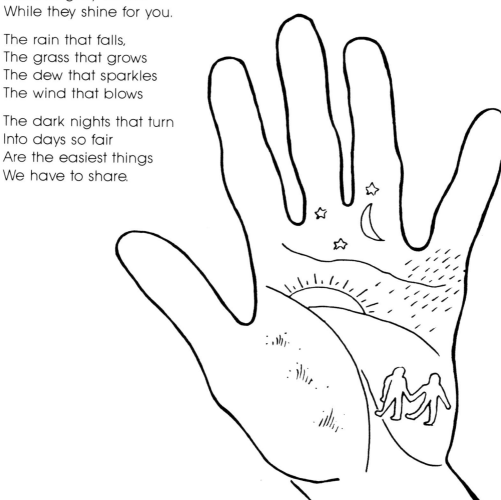

first grade

I am going to first grade
And I know what to do.
My big sister told me.
Listen and I'll tell you.

I'm going to raise my hand high
Whenever I can't see.
And I'll bring a lot of pennies
Because the milk is not for free.

I'll have to be real quiet
And mind the teacher every day.
And I'll never pester the big kids
When I go outside to play.

Sometimes I might feel kind of scared
But the teacher's going to wink,
And after just a little while
The teacher will help me think.

Inspired by Bernie Cimini

I'll think about some numbers —
All about how they can grow.
I'll think about some colors —
All about what they can show.

I'll think about some people
And some horses and more stuff.
My sister says that sometimes
Thinking hard gets pretty tough.

But if I try to do my best
Right from the very start,
If I listen really good
And I always do my part,

My sister will tell me more
About what I'm supposed to do.
My sister is very smart, you know.
My sister is in grade two!!

17

help !!!

I'm trying hard to learn to read
But what's a kid to do
When there's a NO and a GO and a SO and a HO
And then there's a word like TO?

Reading BONE and CONE and LONE and TONE
Can almost be kind of fun,
But I get upset when I have to believe
That D-O-N-E spells DONE!

It's plain to see a kid like me
Sure needs a helping hand.
No matter how much I really try
I just don't understand.

I'm trying hard to learn to read.
Somehow that's what I'll do,
But for now if you'll just read to me
Someday I'll read to you.

Inspired by Dorsey Hammond

musicolor

Sometimes when the music plays
I close my eyes and listen,
And way down deep inside of me
Things start to glow and glisten.

Blues and purples start to swell,
Break up and dance together.
Then dusty pink comes swirling through,
Floating gently like a feather.

Falling streaks of silver rain
Make puddles round like the moon,
And suddenly reds and yellows
Shout a very different tune.

The melody goes on and on
Like colorful wind that blows,
And when I open up my eyes
I'm the only one who knows

That sometimes when the music plays
I close my eyes and listen,
And way down deep inside of me
Things start to glow and glisten.

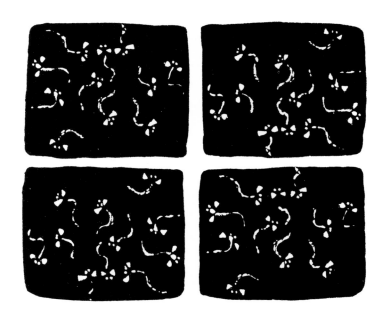

fireflies

When I looked outside late last night
I got the best surprise.
A game of tag was going on
Between some fireflies.

Little lights against the night
Made pictures of the play.
The fireflies all seemed to be
Little fireworks on display.

trees

Trees are very nice to know.
They like to do good things,
Like spread their cooling shade around
And hold up nests and swings.

Trees can be such fun to climb.
They like to sing in the breeze.
Some even give us fruit to eat
And flowers that make us sneeze.

They're dewy in the morning,
Kind of lacey late at night.
When their shadows fall around
It can give you such a fright.

Some trees are tall and powerful.
Some always seem to be weeping.
It's impossible to figure out
When they're awake or sleeping.

Trees can be like people
With big elbows and bony knees.
Some last only a short time.
Some last for centuries.

Trees can stay the same year round
Or change their heads each season.
I like every one of them,
Each for a different reason.

things i'd like to know

Hey, wait for me little butterfly.
You're always gently rushing by —
Fluttering here, fluttering there,
On your way to everywhere.

Before you catch a summer breeze
Or try to make a flower sneeze,
Quick, before you have to go,
There are some things I'd like to know.

Have you ever wished upon a star?
What's it like to travel far?
Do you try hard not to ever fight?
Are you scared when it's very dark at night?

Are the clouds your favorite picture show?
Do you wonder if you'll ever grow?
Have you ever lost your very best friend?
Do you hate to hear a story end?

When the wind blows do you sing along?
Even though you're small are you brave and strong?
When you grow up what do you want to be?
For now, would you like to be friends with me?

outer space

In outer space I'd like to stay
Millions and billions of miles away.

So I could turn my stereo
Way up as loud as it can go.

Where I'd stay up and read all night
And never hear, "Turn out the light!"

Where cookie crumbs would float away
With my dirty socks every single day.

No carrots or liver would I eat
Or ever wear shoes upon my feet.

There'd be no yard of leaves to rake,
Garbage to dump or baths to take,

Tables to set or dishes to dry
And no mean kids to make me cry.

Homework I would never do.
My favorite toys would stay brand new.

All day long I'd have my own way.
I'd say everything I want to say.

I wouldn't have a bed to make.
No vitamins would I have to take.

And I'd never have to share the phone
Because I'd be there all . . . . ALONE?!

color talk

"Hello!", calls yellow.
"Good-bye.", weeps blue.
Shiny red yells, "I love you!"

Lavender sighs, "I'm lazy."

Purple bellows, "I'm strong!"
Orangey-pink announces, "It's dawn!"

Green beckons, "I'm friendly."
Gray whispers "I'm shy."
Playful colors shout, "We're a rainbow!", in the sky.

the diners

The diners ate in slow motion,
Hardly making a sound.
They just kept on with their eating,
Occasionally looking around.

As the sun started down each retired
For the night, to sleep without snore.
I conclude even with an occasional moo
A cow's life is really a bore.

the mouse

That little mouse
Just scared me so
When he ran
Across my toe.

But when he jumped
Upon my knee
He took the breath
Away from me.

It happened fast
As I recall,
Though I was big,
The mouse so small,

I still don't know
While that mouse stayed
Which one of us
Was more afraid.

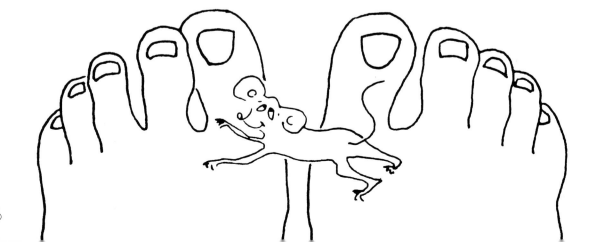

late at night

It's hard to go to sleep at night
When shadows on the wall
Look like ghosts and terrible monsters
And giants ten feet tall.

When the wind is loudly howling
And it's whistling all around,
Your skin gets lots of goose bumps
And your heart just has to pound!

If rain begins to hit the roof
And shakes the window pane,
You're sure it's really some creature
Just too horrible to explain.

You try so hard to get to sleep
Or you'll surely die of fright,
When the next thing that you notice
Is a little speck of light.

It starts out in the corner,
Then it spreads across the floor.
What a relief! It's finally morning
And there's nothing to fear anymore.

That is until some rainy night
When shadows on the wall
Look like ghosts and terrible monsters
And giants ten feet tall!

can you believe it?

While walking to school the other day
I found this note along the way.
It's written to Captain Kangaroo.
I think it'll be a surprise to you!

Oh, Dear Captain Kangaroo,

Each morning we sure do miss you.
We miss your songs, the books you shared,
The way you made us feel you cared
About the things we did and thought —
Even about the colds we caught.
You knew that sometimes we felt sad
And reminded us things weren't so bad.
From farms to castles we traveled and then
You made us glad to be home again.
We think about you and want you to know
We'll always love you wherever you go.
And one thing more I must tell you —
Our kids all miss you as much as we do.

Can you believe it?

how come?

If teachers really already know
What the answers are supposed to be,
How come instead of telling
They're always asking kids like me?

the fawn

In the cool of the morning
I was startled to see
A still silent fawn
Carefully looking at me.

He stared and he stared
As he stood by the tree
And the breeze introduced us,
The fawn and me.

We dared not move,
Not a blink, not a yawn.
As the silence held us
We shared the dawn.

cats

Cats are really clever!
They hardly make a sound
Getting into mischief
Or chasing round and round.

Some cats like to snuggle,
Though some are quite aloof.
Some cats get attention
By climbing on the roof.

Cats are fancy steppers.
They like to skip and dance.
It's like being at the ballet
When a cat begins to prance.

Cats can be so lazy.
It's pretty safe to say
That they like nothing better
Than lounging through the day.

Cats keep many secrets
Hidden in their eyes.
They never will betray you
Or tell you foolish lies.

Cats may be quite different
According to their fur,
But every cat's the same
When it comes down to a purrrrrrr.

why?

I spent all night on my homework.
I did it all by myself.
I tucked it inside my notebook
And carefully set it down on the shelf.

I **woke** up before the alarm rang,
Got ready and went to school.
I wanted to get there early
So I didn't even stop to fool.

When homework was being collected
I was feeling so proud of myself
That I didn't realize 'til that moment
My homework was home on the shelf!

How come when I try my hardest
To do what I'm supposed to do
Something always seems to go wrong?
Does this ever happen to you?

not now

I don't want to know why the rain falls
But I do like the feeling of wet.
I don't understand why the sun shines
But I love the warm feeling I get.
I don't care how oceans can make clouds
But soft pictures in the sky make me smile.
Maybe someday I'll learn all about that stuff
But not for a long long while.

the sneeze

Everytime I have to sneeze
I try real hard to hold it.
I pinch my nose and grit my teeth
In an effort to control it.

I close my eyes and hold my breath.
I feel as though I'm choking.
Trying to keep from sneezing
Is a matter not for joking!

I stand up on my tiptoes
And I hum a little tune.
Still the sneeze inside keeps growing
Like air stretching a balloon.

I put my fingers in my ears
Then get down on my knees,
And after doing all these things
You guessed it — I still sneeze!

I know I cannot stop it
But there's one thing I can do —
Decide if the sneeze is going to be
Ah'choo!, Aaaaaaaaaaaahhh-choo!

or Ah-choOOOOOOOOOO!

Not to be able to stop a sneeze
Is really no surprise,
So I think I'm just going to concentrate
On sneezing with open eyes!

the secret

When lying in bed
Trying to sleep
Do you ever wonder, too,
Just exactly what it is
That Katy-did
Or didn't do?

All night long
The chant goes on.
I guess nobody knows.
The more I try
To figure it out,
The more the mystery grows.

Now if some day
You should find out
Katy's secret — don't tell me,
Because I love making up
All sorts of things
That it could possibly be.

And if at night
When trying to sleep
You like guessing games to play,
Here's something else
To think about —
Who is Katy, anyway??

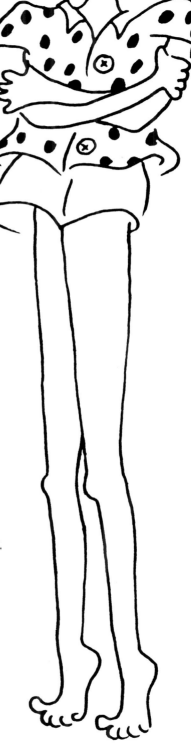

a baby-sitter?

Oh Mom, who needs a baby-sitter?
A baby, that's who, not me!
I'm big enough to stay home alone
As you can plainly see.

When are you going to understand
I'm not a little kid anymore?
I'm old enough to take care of myself.
This is getting to be such a bore.

With windows locked and the drapes closed
I'll be alright all alone.
I won't open the door if anyone knocks.
I promise not to fool on the phone.

I'll read a good book — a murder mystery.
On second thought, maybe not.
T.V. is showing THE GRAVE ROBBERS.
Noooooo, I think T.V. will make the room too hot.

I don't think I'll mind the wierd noises,
Or the shadows on the wall late at night,
Or the sound of the wind willdly howling.
I'm sure I'm going to be alright.

But if it really means all that much to you
Thinking of how alone I will be,
If it's going to spoil your whole evening
Oh, go ahead — call a sitter for me.

haircut

I hate to get my haircut!
It's very humiliating
To have to sit and get stared at
By strangers who are waiting.

Why do I need lots of haircuts?
Isn't once a year enough
To have to get wrapped in a bed sheet
And get sprayed with that gross smelly stuff?

I'll never forget my first haircut,
How the tears rolled down my cheeks.
It looked like somebody mowed my head!
I wouldn't go outside for weeks.

The worst thing about a haircut
Is to think that I have to pay
Someone who calmly smiles and talks
While I'm getting snipped away.

amazing!

Plant a teeny tiny seed
Early in the spring.
When summer comes
Just watch the way
That seed will do its thing!

commotion

I heard a gentle commotion.
I wondered what it could be.
When I ran to look I was breathless
At the sight of what waited for me.

The flower garden was blooming
With sounds I had never heard.
My heart joined in with the harmony
That came with the song of a bird.

I sat and listened a long time
To this melody I had found,
And to this day I remember
Each and every colorful sound.

nightmare

A terrible thing happened to me.
It scared me half to death.
When it was over I was shaking.
I had nearly lost my breath.

Fractions chased me down the hall.
I didn't know what to do.
And worst of all I stumbled
On a remainder of thirty-two!

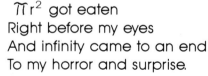

When I added I got the difference!
When I substracted I got the sum!
I forgot how to divide and multiply!
I was feeling so awful and dumb.

Then all the square roots turned to circles
And rolled on down the street.
I couldn't even tell the difference
Between inches, yards and feet!

πr^2 got eaten
Right before my eyes
And infinity came to an end
To my horror and surprise.

If something like this should happen to you
Don't worry — It'll be alright.
The only time it will happen
Is in the middle of the night.

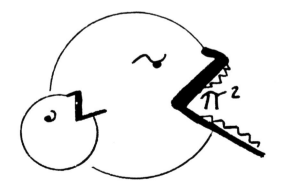

who knows?

People are always asking me,
"When you grow up what do you want to be?"
Now take me very seriously
Because I've thought about it carefully,
And after considering each possibility
I just don't know yet, truthfully.
But I will tell you honestly,
Quite frankly and unequivocally,
The one thing I will never be
Is a person who always asks kids like me,
"When you grow up what do you want to be?"

Maybe I'll be a ballet dancer
Or an astronaut.
Who knows?

recess

We were playing.
It was fun.
Running and jumping — everyone.

And up above
On a playground of blue
Some birds were out at recess, too.

when my dog died

When my dog died
I cried and I cried.
I felt all empty
Way down deep inside.

I couldn't sleep.
I hardly ate.
In school it was hard
To concentrate.

I kept remembering
Things we had done,
The messes we made.
We had so much fun.

I laughed out loud
When I thought of the day
My silly old dog
Scared the salesman away.

I missed her most
When I went to bed.
I cried and I prayed
That she wouldn't be dead.

My dad understood
When I laughed and cried.
He told me about
When his dog had died.

He said every day
Wouldn't be quite so bad.
That I'd never forget
But I'd get over the sad.

What my dad said is true.
My heart is at rest.
And I'll always remember
My dog was the best.

clocks

Clocks must get awfully tired
Having hands that only go around.
And it's probably very monotonous
Making the same old ticking sound.

Just once if clocks could wave their hands
And had silly things to say,
They'd certainly have a lot of fun
Making a mess of our whole day.

morning

"It's time to get up."
        "I don't wanna."
"It's time to get dressed."
        "I don't care."
"It's time to eat."
        "I'm not hungry."
"It's Saturday."
        "Hey, THAT'S NOT FAIR!"

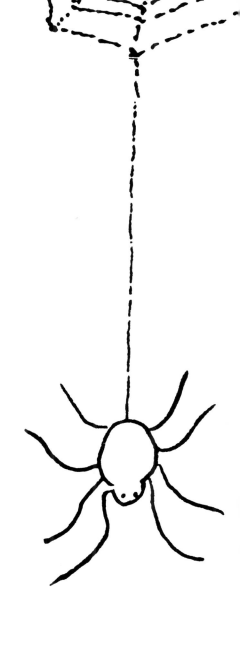

wondering

Sometimes when I have nothing to do,
I wonder how spiders do what they do.
When they go climbing up the wall
I wonder why they do not fall.
When crossing a ceiling up side down
They never tumble to the ground.
I can't figure out where spiders hide
That thread they use when they need a ride.
When spiders stay a while in a place,
How do they leave that gift of lace?
How come a spider so little and gray
Can frighten and scare big people away?
Sometimes when spiders have nothing to do,
I wonder if they wonder about me, too.

43

animals understand

If kids could talk to animals
Like elephants and mice,
I know we'd have a good old time —
Animals never give advice.

"Comb your hair! Brush your teeth!
Clean your room right now!",
Are words that kids would never hear
If talking with a cow.

"Eat your beans! Pull up your socks!
In school don't fool or fight!"
These are words kids hear a lot,
Like morning, noon and night!

How come grown-ups just can't see
Little kids are pretty nice,
And all that little kids really need
Is very little advice?!

sounds in the night

I heard it! I heard it!
It was a little squeak.
I pulled the covers over my head
And then I heard a creak.
I put the pillow on my face.
That's when I heard a bump.
And when I crawled underneath the bed
I know I heard a thump.
There were cracks and snaps
And thuds and slaps.
I yelled 'cause it got so bad.
When I opened my eyes
Was I happy to see
The feet of my mom and dad!
They pulled me out and held me tight.
There were no monsters, not even a mouse.
Mom and Dad said what I heard
Was just the symphony of our house.

if

If the moon came up in the morning
And the sun came out at night,
Would stars grow like little flowers?
Would flowers make the sky color bright?

If the clouds rolled around the big fields
And the sky became fields of brown,
Would the rain then have to fall upwards?
Would it make a lot of mud fall down?

If I went to bed in my school cothes
And I went to school in p.j.'s,
Would I get to think through the night?
Would I get to dream through the day?

If all the kids became grown-ups
And each grown-up turned into a kid,
Would kids understand grown-up thinking?
Would grown-ups recall things they once did?

flower talk

Brand new little flowers
Seem to know just where they're going,
And when the sun is in the sky
They get so busy growing.

Sometimes their heads get droopy
And one rests against another.
I think that's when they're telling
Deep dark secrets to each other.

When tiny gentle raindrops
Fall upon each eager flower,
If you listen very carefully
You'll hear singing in the shower.

And the petals when unfolded
With such colors sure to please,
Will send out the glad announcement
On a warm and gentle breeze.

moon games

When the moon hides behind a cloud
Or goes in and out and through,
It's as if the moon is playing
Hide-and-seek or peek-a-boo.

When the moon seems to be shrinking,
Getting smaller in the sky,
It's like someone's scooping spoonsful
From a great big ice cream pie.

I like the moon best of all
When it looks like a friendly face.
I think it's up there smiling
Because it's found someone to chase.

new kid

Being the new kid is awful!
It's very embarrassing, too,
When everyone's always watching
To see what you're going to do.

Tripping and dropping my lunch tray,
Spilling paint all over the floor
Weren't nearly as disasterous as the day
I opened the wrong bathroom door!

And every time I get called on
My tongue and my braces collide.
Why is this happening to me?
I wish I could just go and hide.

It really wasn't that funny
When someone put gum on my seat.
Everyone heard the teacher say
That she thinks I'm very sweet!!!

I know I'm sure to get noticed
Whenever I make a mistake.
How much more can I take of this?
Won't somebody give me a break?

Each day I get up and I wonder
What new horrors I'll have to face.
I wish I could just be an old kid
And some new kid would come take my place!

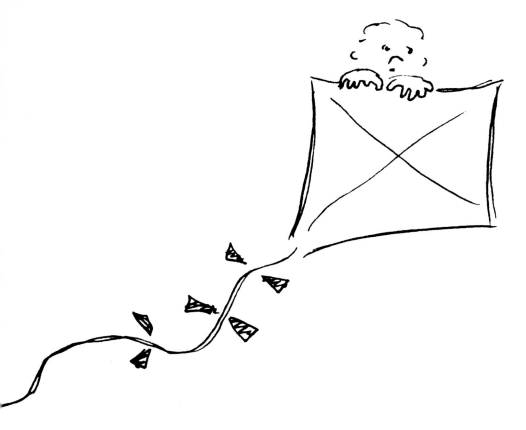

right again!

My mom says, "You're a dreamer."
My dad says, "You're so slow."
My sister says, "You're such a pest.
Get out of here. Just go!"
My teacher says, "You're messy."
The kids say, "Go fly a kite."
My grandmother says, "You're a special child."
I think my grandmother's right!

overworked

Teacher!
    I'm so tired I could sigh
    Inside out
    From my head to my toes.
    Nobody knows.

Teacher!
    I'm so tired I could cry
    Right out loud,
    Sob and screech
    While you teach.

Teacher!
    I'm so tired I could die
    Here, now,
    Fall out of my chair.
    Would you care?

Teacher!
    I'm so tired
    Because you got hired.
    My only hope
    Is if you get fired!

puddles

When grown-ups see a puddle
They carefully step around,
But kids just walk right through
Because they love that splashy sound.

Jumping right in the middle
Is the very best thing to do.
Grown-ups don't know what they're missing.
If they did, they'd jump in, too!

new snow

When snow is newly fallen
I go walking and I find
No matter how far I go forward
Some of me always gets left behind.

rainy days

I hate it when it's raining
And I can't go out to play.
Parents just don't understand
Rain makes a perfect day

For jumping into puddles
And for pies of mud and grass.
Instead, they say, "Be patient, dear,
This shower will quickly pass."

So I quietly watch at the window
When I could be out in the rain,
And I think of all the fun times
That are going down the drain!

early in the morning

Early on a cool clear morning
When the world is still asleep,
I like to watch the lazy sun yawn
And slowly start to creep

Across the field and through the trees
Like syrup running thick,
Then slowly spread across the lake
With care so it won't stick.

As it tiptoes through the green grass,
I get ready in my very own space.
I close my eyes and patiently wait
For the sun to reach my face.

It's one of my favorite things to do
And even when it is cloudy and gray,
All I have to do is close my eyes
And remember a sunshiny day.

(?????????)

whereareyouwhenI'mneedingyou
likethisafternoonatquarterpasttwo?

I said!

WHEREAREYOUWHENI'MNEEDINGYOU
LIKETHISAFTERNOONATQUARTERPASTTWO?

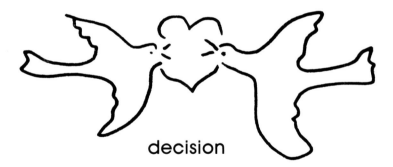

decision

Why do we have to play battle?
Why do we have to play war?
What's annihilation, anyway?
Playing's not much fun anymore.

One side must "kill off" the other
Because only one side can be best.
Should I try to think up a better game
Or leave fighting to all the rest?

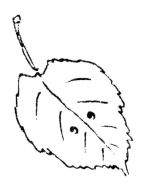

farewell

The grass shivered when the wind passed by,
The message was very clear.
The flowers drooped in their gentle way.
The birds swarmed and then flew away.
Evening snatched an extra piece of day.
Summer was gone for another year.

index